The Cat Says Meow
Caring for Your Cat for Kids
Pet Books for Kids
Children's Animal Care & Pets Books

pfiffikus

EDUCATIONAL BOOKS FOR CHILDREN K-12

Cats are some of the most lovable animals in the world. Read on to know how to take care of your pet cats.

Take your cat to the veterinarian for checkups.

If you have kittens, take them to the veterinarian for vaccinations.

If your cat becomes sick, take her to the veterinarian for medical treatment.

Have your cat spayed to prevent diseases like cancer and mammary gland tumors.

Give your cat a bath only when they are dirty.

If you cat
has long fur,
brush it.

Grooming is very important because it stimulates your cat's blood flow.

Brush your cat's teeth using a soft-bristled brush and veterinary-recommended toothpaste.

Dental care is very important because bad bacteria may enter your cat's bloodstream and invade the rest of its body.

Create a comfortable and private space for your cat.

Ask your
veterinarian
what food
your cat
needs to eat.

Cats need foods derived from animals because they are carnivores.

Always let your pet cat drink fresh water, and not milk.

Feed your pet regularly.

Play with
your pet
every day.

Your cat should
have an object
to play with
to prevent
boredom.

Allow your cat to play with her food to keep her active especially if she is an indoor cat.

Cats may look like independent animals but they also need some care. Show your cat that you love her. Take care of her every day!

Made in the USA
Columbia, SC
10 December 2018